1 MONTH OF
FREE
READING

at
www.ForgottenBooks.com

By purchasing this book you are eligible for one month membership to ForgottenBooks.com, giving you unlimited access to our entire collection of over 700,000 titles via our web site and mobile apps.

To claim your free month visit:
www.forgottenbooks.com/free281462

ISBN 978-0-656-78675-6
PIBN 10281462

This book is a reproduction of an important historical work. Forgotten Books uses state-of-the-art technology to digitally reconstruct the work, preserving the original format whilst repairing imperfections present in the aged copy. In rare cases, an imperfection in the original, such as a blemish or missing page, may be replicated in our edition. We do, however, repair the vast majority of imperfections successfully; any imperfections that remain are intentionally left to preserve the state of such historical works.

CATALOGUE OF THE OFFICERS AND STUDENTS

...OF...

Maryville College

TENNESSEE

FOR THE YEAR
1898–99

PHILADELPHIA
MacCalla & Company Inc., Printers
237-9 Dock Street
1899

Board of Directors.

✄ ✄ ✄

CLASS OF 1899.

Rev. E. A. Elmore, D.D.,

Rev. R. L. Bachman, D.D.,

Rev. J. H. McConnell,

Rev. J. C. Lord,

Rev. W. A. Ervin,

Rev. J. T. Cooter,

Rev. Thomas Lawrence, D.D.,

Rev. Nathan Bachman, D.D.,

Hon. W. A. McTeer,

W. B. Minnis,

A. R. McBath, Esq.,

Jos. A. Muecke.

CLASS OF 1900.

Rev. W. J. Trimble, D.D.,

Rev. C. A. Duncan, D.D.,

Rev. J. W. C. Willoughby, D.D.,

Rev. J. E. Alexander, D.D.,

Rev. A. J. Clark,

Rev. C. B. Lord,

Rev. W. R. Dawson,

Rev. John S. Eakin,

Hon. W. L. Brown,

Col. John B. Minnis,

Ben Cunningham,

T. G. Montague.

CLASS OF 1901.

Rev. Jere Moore, D.D.,

Rev. W. H. Lyle, D.D.,

Rev. H. P. Cory,

Rev. W. H. Lester, Jr.,

Rev. A. J. Coile,

Rev. W. H. Franklin,

Rev. J. M. Alexander,

Rev. Arno Moore,

Hon. W. P. Washburn,

John C. McClung,

Judge John P. Smith,

J. P. Hooke, Esq.

Rev. W. H. LYLE, D.D.,
President.

Major BEN CUNNINGHAM,
Recorder.

Hon. W. A. McTEER,
Treasurer.

ᚠaculty

❧ ❧ ❧

Rev. SAMUEL W. BOARDMAN, D.D., LL.D.,
> President, and Professor of Mental and Moral
> Science and of Didactic Theology.

Rev. SAMUEL T. WILSON, D.D.,
> Professor of the English Language and Litera-
> ture and of the Spanish Language.

Rev. ELMER B. WALLER, A.M.,
> . . . . Professor of Mathematics.

Rev. HERMAN A. GOFF, A.M.,
> Professor in the Department of Mathematics,
> Registrar and Librarian.

JAMES H. M. SHERRILL, A.M.,
> Professor of the Greek Language and Literature.

GEO. S. FISHER, Ph.D.,
> . . . . Professor of the Natural Sciences.

JASPER C. BARNES, A.M.,
> Principal of the Preparatory Department and
> Professor of the Science and Art of Teaching.

Rev. JOHN G. NEWMAN, A.M.,
> Professor of the Latin Language and Literature.

FRANK M. GILL,
. . *Instructor in the Preparatory Department.*

Miss MARGARET E. HENRY,
. . *Instructor in the Preparatory Department.*

Miss LEILA M. PERINE, Mus.B.,
. . . . . . *Instructor on the Piano and Organ.*

Miss AMANDA LAUGHLIN ANDREWS, B.Ph.,
. . . . . . *Instructor in French and German.*

HORACE L. ELLIS, A.B.,
. . *Instructor in the Preparatory Department.*

CARL H. ELMORE, A.B.,
. . *Instructor in the Preparatory Department.*

ISAAC ALLISON GAINES, A.M.,
Instructor in English Language and Literature.

Mrs. HELEN H. SANFORD,
. . . . *Matron.*

WILLIAM THOMAS,
. . . . *Janitor.*

Mrs. A. A. WILSON,
Manager of the Coöperative Boarding Club.

Miss H. M. KINGSBURY,
Assistant Matron and Assistant Manager of the Coöperative Boarding Club.

STUDENTS.

College Department.

Senior Class.

Classical Course.

CARNAHAN, MARY GAINES, . . . Maryville.
LYLE, HUBERT SAMUEL, ... Dandridge.
McMURRAY, SAMUEL DUFFIELD, . . Mt. Horeb.
MAGILL, CHARLES NEWTON, . . . Maryville.
POST, RICHARD WALTER, ... St. Andrews Bay, Fla.
WELSH, HOWARD MARTIN, ... Lincoln.

Philosophical Course.

ALEXANDER, MARY ELLEN, . . . Brick Mill.
KENNEDY, ETHEL MEEK, ... Knoxville.
LYLE, ROSE MIRIAM, ... Dandridge.
SMYTHE, PHI, ... Carringer.

Latin Scientific Course.

LITTERER, CHARLES CONRAD, . . . Danville, Pa.

Junior Class.

Classical Course.

CALDWELL, FREDERICK CHARLES, . . New Market.
CUNNINGHAM, CLAY, ... Maryville.
ELLIS, EDWIN LINK, ... Maryville.
ELMORE, ROBERT BARTLETT, . . . Knoxville.
ERVIN, MORTON WAYNE, ... Wartburg.
McCONNELL, THOMAS HEATHERINGTON, . Wilmington, O.
RAMSEY, WILLIAM THOMAS, . . . Manchester, O.
REED, GEORGE WILLIAM, ... Grassy Cove.
RIMMER, HARVEY CAWOOD, . . . Dandridge.

Philosophical Course.

LORD, HENRIETTA MILLS, ... Maryville.
MINNIS, ETHEL BIDDLE, ... New Market.
NEWMAN, EDITH L., ... Piedmont.

Sophomore Class.

Classical Course.

BARTLETT, WILLIAM THAW, . . . Maryville.
BOYD, MARTIN LUTHER, ... Maryville.
CAMPBELL, WILLIAM ALBERT EDWARD, . Kitchen, O.
MAGUIRE, THOMAS, ... Manchester, England.
MISER, SAMUEL THOMAS, ... Maryville.
PFLANZE, LOUIS, ... Maryville.

Philosophical Course.

ALEXANDER, EMMA, ... Tokio, Japan.
HENRY, CHARLES WILLIAM, . . . Maryville.

Freshman Class.

Classical Course.

BRAZELTON, JAMES HENRY AUGUSTUS, . New Market.
ERVIN, HELEN ELAINE, ... Wartburg.
GODDARD, ARTHUR BRIAN, ... Maryville.
HAMILTON, HERBERT THEOPHILUS, . . Fayetteville.
HARMON, WILLIAM EDGAR, . . . Eusebia.
HULL, ARTHUR GIBSON, ... Maryville.
PENNEY, ELIZABETH, ... Perryville, Ky.
SABIN, WILLIAM ROBERTSON, . . . Johnson City.
TRACY, JOHN EVARTS, ... Crossville.
WALKER, WALLACE ALLEN, . . . Macomb, Ill.
WEBB, FREDERIC LEE, ... Cincinnati, O.

Philosophical Course.

JOHNSTON, GRACE MAY, ...   Blue Ash, O.
LORD, HARRIET CECILIA, ...   Maryville.
RISEDEN, WILLIAM, ...   Wartburg.
STEBBINS, MAME, ...   Grand View.

Scientific Course.

FEAGLES, HARRY, ...   Cutler, Ill.
GARNER, HENRY EDWARD, ...   McKinley.
McCROSKEY, ADA FRANCES,   .   .   .   Glenlock.

Irregular.

BROYLES, LUCIE BELLE, ...   Maryville.
CALDWELL, RICHARD MILTON,   .   .   .   Maryville.
CANADA, LAUNCE, ...   Winchester, Ind.
CARNAHAN, CLARA GRACE, ...   Maryville.
COLBERT, JOHN WILLIAM, ...   Sao Paulo, Brazil.
COXE, ADELIA MAE, ...   New Market.
DYMOND, JACOB FRANKLIN,   .   .   .   Beaumont, Pa.
GILL, MARY BELLE, ...   Maryville.
HASTINGS, MARY LENA, ...   Maryville.
HENDRICKS, DOCKTOR FRANK,   .   .   .   Field, S. C.
HOWARD, CORNELIA JANE,   .   .   .   Maryville.
KIDD, ADDIE EMILY, ...   Maryville.
MUECKE, FREDERICA, ...   Kingston.
POST, ALFRED ANDREWS, ...   St. Andrews Bay, Fla.
SMITH, WILLIAM BRYAN, ...   Woodville, Ga.
TOOLE, WALLACE OTIS, ...   Maryville.
TURNBULL, JOHN WALLACE,   .   .   .   Cambridge, N. Y.

Music Only.

ANDREWS, ELLEN, ...   Butler, Pa.
ANDREWS, PEARL, ...   Butler, Pa.
GARNER, HERMAN, ...   Maryville.
GOFF, MARY, ...   Maryville.
HUDDLESTON, ALBERT, ...   Maryville.

Teachers' Course.

Third Year.

ACUFF, BERT HOWARD, ...	Washburne.
CURTIS, CORA MAE, ...	Cliff.
GAMBLE, MALLIE, ...	Maryville.
GAMBLE, MAYME, ...	Maryville.
HOOD, LILLIAN, ...	Knoxville.
McCAMPBELL, EDITH AYRTON, . . .	Knoxville.
MAGILL, JESSIE RANKIN, ...	Maryville.
STOFFELL, SALLIE ESTELLA, . . .	Rita.
WILSON, JAMES DAVID, ...	Clover Hill.

Second Year.

CORNETT, LYDIA, ...	Poor Fork, Ky.
CROOK, JULIA LOUISA, ...	New Market.
HALL, CHARLES OSCAR, ...	Flenniken.
RANKIN, ORA IDA, ...	Mt. Horeb.
SEATON, AMOS ALFRED, ...	Maryville.
SHERROD, LINNIE EUDORA, . . .	Knoxville.

First Year.

JONES, ARTHUR BROWN, ...	Chandler.
NUCHOLS, MARY ELIZABETH, . . .	Seaton.

STUDENTS.

Preparatory Department.

Senior Class.

Classical Course.

ALEXANDER, EDWIN CRAWFORD, . . .	Elizabethton.
BACON, JAMES BLAINE, . . .	Pates Hill.
BELK, THURLOW WELLINGTON, . : .	Altan, N. C.
BOARDMAN, MARTHA TRACY, . . .	Maryville.
BROADY, JOSEPH MCCLELLAN, . . .	Maryville.
CRAWFORD, DENNIS WHITE, . : .	Maryville.
CRAWFORD, HUGH RANKIN, . . .	Maryville.
ERNEST, GEORGE, ...	Macomb, Ill.
GARDNER, NANCY VIRGINIA, . . .	Salyersville, Ky.
GIBSON, HENRY KING, ...	South Charleston, O.
GODDARD, HORACE MAYNARD, . . .	Maryville.
GRAU, EDWIN LYSANDER, ...	Knoxville.
JONES, ISAAC WILLIAM, ...	Samsonville, O.
KITCHEN, ERASMUS JONES, ...	Pitchin, O.
MCCLUNG, CARRIE GRAHAM, . . .	Maryville.
MCELWEE, FRANK BROWN, ...	Rockford.
MCMURRY, ANDREW RUSSELL, . . .	Maryville.
MORTON, ALEXANDER WELLS, . . .	Seaton.

Philosophical Course.

ATKINS, LENA, ...	Maryville.
GODDARD, MABEL OLIVE, ...	Flenniken.
HAMMON, JAMES HENRY, ...	Maryville.
KEYES, ARTHUR WASHINGTON, . . .	Crossville.
MUNDY, CARRIE ELMA, ...	Maryville.
PARKER, HOWARD ROBERTS, . . .	Caswell.
RITTER, HENRY FRANCIS, ...	Dutch.
SEYMOUR, HENRY TILDEN, ...	Dutch.

Scientific Course.

CONING, FRANK WILLIAM, ... Maryville.
FRENCH, CHARLES ALEXANDER, . . . Bank.
FRYE, ALDINE BURDETTE, ... Maryville.
HAFLEY, HORACE CHARLES, . . . Maryville.

Middle Class.

Classical Course.

BROWN, CECIL BAYARD, ... Philadelphia.
BROWN, THOMAS GUTHRIE, ... Philadelphia.
DICKIE, PAUL RUPERT, ... Cleveland.
FRANKLIN, MABEL LUCY, ... Grand View.
GODDARD, GRACE, ... Maryville.
JONES, WILLIAM ROWLAND, . . . Ebenezer, Wales.
LAUGHEAD, FRANK EDMUND, . . . Flat Rock, Ill.
LILLARD, JASPER WASHINGTON, . . . Maryville.
PATE, JOSEPH BENJAMIN, ... Maryville.
RICHARDSON, JOHN DARIUS, . . . Maryville.
SEARLE, JOSEPH HUBBARD, ... Grand View.
WALLACE, JOHN QUINCY, ... Soddy.

Philosophical Course.

ALEXANDER, LOIS, ... Tokio, Japan.
ATKINS, EFFIE LEE, ... Maryville.
BRYAN, CLEMMIE MAUD, ... Maryville.
DE LOZIER, MARGARET INA, . . . Bank.
GILL, VENORAH ELIZABETH, . . . Maryville.
GODDARD, MARY FREDDIE, . . . Maryville.
GRIFFITTS, MIKE, ... Kizers.
HAFLEY, ESTELLE, ... Maryville.
HUFFSTETLER, EFFIE, ... Maryville.
PFLANZE, ROBERT, ... Maryville.
POST, HELEN MIRIAM, ... St. Andrews Bay, Fla.
PHILLIPS, LINDSAY BRASSFIELD, . . . Huntsville.
WEBB, EUGENE LESLIE, ... Cincinnati, O.

Scientific Course.

DE LOZIER, NELLIE, ... Bank.
MCCAMPBELL, HARVEY BENNETT, . . Beverly.
SHERRILL, MARY TEXANNA, . . . Bank.

Junior Class.

Philosophical Course.

ARSTINGSTALL, CARRIE LUCY,	Montgomery, O.
ATKINS, MINNIE ANNA,	Maryville.
BEATTY, READING KEARNS,	Doylestown, Pa.
BIBLE, JESSE,	Ketoville.
BROADY, MABEL MALINDA,	Maryville.
BROADY, NANNIE MOLLIE,	Maryville.
CALDWELL, EMMA ELIZA,	Maryville.
CASTILE, DANIEL,	Asheville, N. C.
EVERETT, WILLIAM THOMAS,	Maryville.
FAGG, PARIS HAYNES,	Maryville.
FLINN, HENRIETTA,	Montgomery, O.
FRANKLIN, MACK CALVIN,	Mt. Horeb.
FRYE, HOMER MEADE,	Maryville.
GEORGE, JAMES MONTGOMERY,	Smithwood.
GEORGE, WALTER ALEXANDER,	Knoxville.
GODDARD, EDWARD TARWATER,	Flenniken.
GODDARD, ILIA BOYNTON,	Maryville.
GODDARD, MAGGIE,	Maryville.
GODDARD, MARTHA,	Maryville.
HACKNEY, CARL LESLIE,	Maryville.
HACKNEY, CHESTER,	Maryville.
HASTINGS, ELLEN PEARL,	Maryville.
HENRY, JAMES ARTHUR,	Maryville.
JOHNSTON, LOU FENTON,	Montgomery, O.
JOHNSTON, WILLIAM MATTHEW,	Indianapolis, Ind.
KENNEDY, WILLIAM HENRY,	Maryville.
LEWIS, WILLIAM E.,	Peely, Pa.
McCLUNG, DENNIE,	Maryville.
McREYNOLDS, GRACE ELINOR,	Maryville.
McTEER, WILLIAM SAMUEL,	Maryville.
MAGILL, ANNIE McCLURE,	Maryville.
MAYS, ADDISON WESLEY,	Winstead.
MIKELS, COWAN SYLVESTER,	Knoxville.
MIKELS, HUGH OSCAR,	Knoxville.
MUNDY, EDNA McREYNOLDS,	Maryville.
PARHAM, GUY,	Maryville.
PARHAM, WILLIAM RHADAMANTHUS,	Maryville.
PATTON, REYMOND REED,	Maryville.
PFLANZE, OTTO,	Maryville.
PORTER, SAMUEL ANDREW,	Maryville.
QUIST, ELI NATHANAEL,	Norseland, Minn.
RODDY, JOHN MARTIN,	Bank.

STERLING, LUM ALEXANDER, . . .	Maryville.
SUSONG, ALLIE MAY, ...	Maryville.
SUSONG, HERMAN MILTON, ...	Maryville.
SUSONG, WALTER THOMAS, ...	Maryville.
TARWATER, OLIVER VERLIN, . . .	Maryville.
WALKER, DAISY JANE, ...	Cliff.
WALLACE, EVERETT LINUS, . . .	Wilmington, O.
WATT, ARTHUR STERLING, ...	Knoxville.
WEISGERBER, FLORENCE BLANCHE, . .	Bearden.
WHITE, ALBERT TOWNSEND, . . .	Knoxville.

Scientific Course.

ADAMS, NETTIE AMELIA, ...	Knoxville.
ALEXANDER, SARAH EVALINE, . . .	Meadow.
ALEXANDER, THERON, ...	Tokio, Japan.
AMBRISTER, MARY LILLIAN, . . .	Maryville.
AMBRISTER, WILLIE E., ...	Maryville.
AMERINE, MAGGIE, ...	Maryville.
AMERINE, SABRINA EVALINE, . . .	Gamble.
BABCOCK, FREDERICK REUBEN, . . .	St. Andrews Bay, Fla.
BARKER, FESTUS ELMER, ...	Maryville.
BEALS, JOHN CUNNINGHAM, ...	Kizers.
BELK, WILLIAM ARTHUR, ...	Altan, N. C.
BEST, CALEB LEONARD, ...	McKinley.
BEST, WARREN DICKENSON, . . .	McKinley.
BETTIS, CLARA ARMENIA, ...	Mt. Horeb.
BIDDLE, CHARLES MACK, ...	White Pine.
BINGHAM, HANNAH, ...	Concord.
BLANKENSHIP, JOHN HARRIS, . . .	Meadow.
BOND, JOE PORTER, ...	Maryville.
BRADFORD, ROBERT HARRIS, . . .	·Charlotte, N. C.
BRIENT, CHARLES NELSON, ...	Kizers.
BYERLY, HOMER PIERSON, ...	Clover Hill.
CAMERON, BERTHA MAE, ...	Ellejoy.
CAMPBELL, SUSIE, ...	Maryville.
CARPENTER, MAUDE LORENA, . . .	McKinley.
CAVENER, GEORGE EUGENE, . . .	Mohawk.
CHANDLER, RICHARD ALEXANDER, . .	Maryville.
CHANDLER, WILLIAM BENJAMIN, . .	Maryville.
CHAPMAN, MILTON, ...	Meadow.
CLEMENS, WILLIE PEARL, ...	Maryville.
COCHRAN, HATTIE HENRIETTA, . . .	Rockford.
COSTNER, ISAAC CLAUDIUS, ...	Clover Hill.
CRAWFORD, JENNIE FIRDILA, . . .	Maryville.
COULTER, BEN CATLETT, ...	Maryville.

COULTER, FLORENCE,	Maryville.
COWAN, FLORA,	Maryville.
DAVIS, MELVINA,	Maryville.
DILOPOULO, ALEXANDER GEORGE,	Athens, Greece.
DONALDSON, TAYLOR,	Unitia.
DUNCAN, SOPHIA ELIZABETH,	Maryville.
DUNN, CHARLES WINFIELD,	Tuckaleechee.
DUNN, WILLIAM CLAUDE,	Tuckaleechee.
EVERETT, JAMES VINCENT,	Seaton.
EVERETT, MANSON,	Maryville.
FISHER, JEANETTE,	Maryville.
FRANCE, ARTIE BELLE,	Louisville.
FRAZIER, EDWARD,	Gap Creek.
FRENCH, JESSE EDGAR,	Flenniken.
FRENCH, VON OLIVER,	Asbury.
FRYE, CHARLES ORR,	Maryville.
GAMBLE, ANNIE ELIZA,	No Time.
GAMBLE, ANDREW HOUSTON,	No Time.
GAMBLE, DELLA ELIZABETH,	Maryville.
GAMBLE, GEORGE COWAN,	No Time.
GAMBLE, GRACE,	Gamble.
GAMBLE, JOSIAS EDGAR,	Maryville.
GAMBLE, SIDNEY,	Gamble.
GEORGE, FREDERICK,	Maryville.
GIFFIN, WILLIAM DAVID,	Maryville.
GILLESPIE, NONA,	Millers.
GOFF, EARL AUGUSTUS,	Bon Air.
GOFF, EDNA,	Maryville.
GODDARD, BERYL BARUM REBECCA,	Maryville.
GODDARD, JAMES HENRY,	Maryville.
GODDARD, RALEIGH ERNEST,	Maryville.
GODDARD, ROSCOE NATHANAEL,	Maryville.
GODDARD, SAMUEL MONROE,	Maryville.
GODDARD, SARAH ADELINE,	Maryville.
GREER, JOHN HOMER,	Greenback.
GRIFFITTS, GUSSIE,	Unitia.
GULLEDGE, THOMAS ALONZO,	Altan, N. C.
HARMON, CHARLES WALTER,	Maryville.
HARNED, LODUSKA,	Thesha.
HENRY, HORACE BURTON,	Maryville.
HENRY, ZORA ALICE,	Rockford.
HOOD, CHARLES HARRISON,	Knoxville.
HUDDLESTON, OLIVER TERRELL,	Maryville.
HUMPHREY, JACOB COWAN,	Unitia.
HUMPHREY, JACOB HOUSTON,	Gamble.
HUTTON, JOHN WYCLIFFE,	Maryville.

HUTTON, SALLIE STELLA,	Maryville.
IDDINS, CLEMENT McCONNELL,	Maryville.
IDDINS, EDWARD CAMPBELL,	Maryville.
IDDINS, MARY LOUISA,	Maryville.
IRWIN, JOHN BAXTER,	Maryville.
JACKSON, NELLIE SUCKEY,	New Decatur, Ala.
KIDD, ROBERT PAUL,	Maryville.
KIRK, BIRDIE IDELLA,	Maryville.
KIRK, WILLIE HARRISON,	Maryville.
LANEY, JULIAN WALTER,	Altan, N. C.
LAUGHEAD, CHARLES WALTER,	Flat Rock, Ill.
LAWSON, JESSE MITCHELL,	Maryville.
LEQUIRE, GRANVILLE DEXTER,	Nila, Ala.
LEWIS, ROSCOE FREDERICK,	Dail.
LONG, JACOB ABRAHAM,	Block House.
LOWRY, DONALD HENDERSON,	Maryville.
McCALL, JAMES ERNEST,	Knoxville.
McCALL, JOHN FRANKLAND,	Knoxville.
McCAMMON, ARTHUR ROLLIE,	Brick Mill.
McCAMMON, LILLIE FLORENCE,	Brick Mill.
McCLUNG, CARL RUSSELL,	Maryville.
McCONNELL, JENNIE MAY,	Maryville.
McCULLOCH, JOHN CARROLL,	Rockford.
McFARLAND, RUSSELL HENRY,	Elizabethton.
McGINLEY, FLORA EDNA,	Maryville.
McGINLEY, MARGARET LUCINDA,	Maryville.
McGINLEY, MARY,	Maryville.
McGINLEY, MINNIE LOUELLA,	Maryville.
McINTURF, ISRAEL WASHINGTON,	Tuckaleechee.
McKENZIE, INA BELLE,	Maryville.
McKENZIE, LIZINKA LEE,	Maryville.
McLEMORE, JOHN BLAINE,	Ford.
McMURRY, ADRA BELLE,	Maryville.
McMURRY, LULA JANE,	Maryville.
McTEER, IRA,	Ellejoy.
McTEER, WILLIAM ARTHUR,	Ellejoy.
MAGILL, EFFIE,	Maryville.
MAGILL, LAURA JANE,	Maryville.
MALLOUK, ELIAS,	New York, N. Y.
MARTIN, BOSE LEE,	Maryville.
MARTIN, JOSEPH MARCELLUS,	Maryville.
MILLSAPS, MARY ANN IDA,	Gamble.
MISTLAN, MONOEL,	Ponce, Porto Rico.
MOORE, GEORGE PORTER,	Cates Cross Roads.
MOORE, PERRY ELISHA,	Shady Grove.
MORTON, MAY,	Maryville.

MORTON, NORA EVA,	Seaton.
MORTON, OCEY MAY,	Maryville.
NASSOUR, KHALIL ABRAHAM,	New York, N. Y.
NEWBERRY, FRED COLUMBUS,	Meadow.
NUCHOLS, LOUANNA,	Seaton.
OLIVER, GEORGE,	Cades Cove.
PARHAM, MARY IRENE,	Maryville.
PARKER, EMERSON DEWEY,	Huntsville.
PATTY, LUZENA DELLA,	Redfield, Ia.
PEDIGO, LULA,	Maryville.
POST, LIDA ANNA,	St. Andrews Bay, Fla.
PRAYTOR, EDWARD BROWN,	Gypsey, N. C.
PROFFITT, FRED LOWRY,	Maryville.
PROFFITT, HARRY HERMAN,	Maryville.
PROFFITT, SANDERS,	Ogles.
RANKIN, WILBUR GARFIELD,	Flat Gap.
RECTOR, ROBERT GAITHER,	Marshall, N. C.
RITTER, WILLIAM SIMEON,	Dutch.
RODGERS, ALICE,	Maryville.
ROGERS, JOHN WRIGHT,	Ellejoy.
ROWE, NELLIE PEARL,	Maryville.
RUBLE, HENRY DAILEY,	Maryville.
RUBLE, JAMES ALBERT,	Maryville.
RUSSELL, CARRIE,	Maryville.
SAULTS, WILLARD H.,	Tang.
SCHIRMER, FRANK CLARENCE,	Tampa, Fla.
SEATON, CHARLES,	Maryville.
SEATON, MAE,	Maryville.
SELF, DAVID EDGAR,	Rockford.
SELF, JOHN PERRY,	Rockford.
STONE, JAMES BASCOM,	Maryville.
STONE, SALLIE,	Maryville.
STONECIPHER, CARRIE,	Wartburg.
STRAIT, DANIEL GUY,	Flenniken.
SUSONG, TOLBERT STEELE,	Maryville.
SWAN, PARKE PURRIS,	Maryville.
TEFFETELLER, COLUMBUS ALEXANDER,	Maryville.
THOMAS, CHARITY GERTRUDE,	Maryville.
THOMAS, HOMER,	Maryville.
THOMAS, JOHNNIE,	Maryville.
THOMAS, WALTER,	Maryville.
WALLER, EMMA GILCHRIST,	Maryville.
WALKER, HENRY,	Maryville.
WALKER, JOSEPH ARTHUR,	Cliff.
WALKER, MARY LOUDORA,	Maryville.
WATERS, MELINDA JANE,	Waters.

Anderson Hall.

WILBURN, DORA, ...	Maryville.
WHITE, CHARLES, ...	Block House.
WILLIAMS, AMANDA, ...	Wartburg.
WILSON, CARL, ...	Maryville.
WILSON, MINNIE DORCAS, ...	Poplar Flats, Ky.
WILSON, RUTH BROWNING, ...	Maryville.
WOOD, SUSIE, ...	Bybee.
WRIGHT, JAMES GARFIELD, ...	Pall Mall.
WRIGHT, SHERMAN TECUMSEH, . . .	Pall Mall.
YATES, MAUDE ALMA, ...	Loudon.
YOUNG, WILLIAM FARICE, ...	Maryville.

Summary.

❧ ❧ ❧

College Department:

Classical Course, ... 32

Philosophical Course, ... 13

Scientific Course, ... 4

Special Studies, ... 22

Preparatory Department:

Classical Course, ... 30

Philosophical Course, ... 73

Scientific Course, ... 189

Teachers' Course, ... 17

Total, ... 380

Synopsis of Courses of Study.

College Department.

Classical Course.	Philosophical Course.	Scientific Course.
FRESHMAN YEAR.	**FRESHMAN YEAR.**	**FRESHMAN YEAR.**
Fall Term.	**Fall Term.**	**Fall Term.**
Livy 4 Herodotus 4 Algebra 5· Biology A 5 Bible and Rhetorical 2	Livy 4 German 4 Algebra 5 Biology A 5 Bible and Rhetorical 2	German 4 Algebra 5 Biology A 5 Psychology 5 Bible and Rhetorical 2
Spring Term.	**Spring Term.**	**Spring Term.**
De Senectute, 4 Thucydides 4 Geometry 4 Biology B 5 (E) English History 3 Bible and Rhetorical 2	De Senectute 4 German 4 Geometry 4 Biology B 5 English History 3 Bible and Rhetorical 2	German 4 Geometry 4 Biology B 5 English History 3 Bible and Rhetorical 2
SOPHOMORE YEAR.	**SOPHOMORE YEAR.**	**SOPHOMORE YEAR.**
Fall Term.	**Fall Term.**	**Fall Term.**
Tacitus 4 (E) Plato 4 (E) Trigonometry 4 Physics A 4–2 Bunyan ; Outlining 2 English Literature 1 German 3 Bible and Rhetorical 2	Tacitus 4 Trigonometry 4 Physics A 4–2 Bunyan ; Outlining 2 English Literature 1 Bible and Rhetorical 2	Trigonometry 4 Physics A 4–2 Bunyan ; Outlining 2 English Literature 1 Latin 5 (E) Greek 5 (E) Spanish 5 (E) French 5 (E) Bible and Rhetorical 2
Spring Term.	**Spring Term.**	**Spring Term.**
Horace 4 (E) Demosthenes 4 (E) Trigonometry 1 mo. 4 An'lytic'l Geom. 4 mos. 4 (E) Physics B 5 (E) Rhetoric A 3 English Literature 3 (E) German 3 Bible and Rhetorical 2 (Latin or Greek required in both terms. 18 hours re- quired.)	Horace 4 (E) Trigonometry 1 mo. 4 An'lytic'l Geom. 4 mos. 4 (E) Physics B 5 Rhetoric A 3 English Literature 3 (E) Bible and Rhetorical 2 (17 hours required.)	Trigonometry 1 mo. 4 An'lytc'l Geom. 4 mos. 4 (E) Physics B 5 Rhetoric A 3 English Literature 3 Latin 5 (E) Greek 5 (E) Spanish 5 (E) French 5 (E) Bible and Rhetorical 2

Classical Course.	Philosophical Course.	Scientific Course.
JUNIOR YEAR.	**JUNIOR YEAR.**	**JUNIOR YEAR.**
Fall Term.	**Fall Term.**	**Fall Term.**
Latin 4 (E)	Latin 4 (E)	Calculus A 4 (E)
Greek 4 (E)	Calculus A 4 (E)	Physics C 4
Calculus A 4 (E)	Physics C 4 (E)	Chemistry A 2-4
Physics C 4 (E)	Chemistry A 2-4	Shakespeare 2 — Milton 2 —
Chemistry A 2-4	Shakespeare 2 — Milton 2 —	one required.
Shakespeare 2 — Milton 2 —	one required.	Logic A 5
one required.	Logic A 5	Rhetoric B 3 (E)
Logic A 5	Rhetoric B 3 (E)	Bible and Rhetorical 2
Rhetoric B 3 (E)	Bible and Rhetorical 2	
German 3		
Bible and Rhetorical 2		
Spring Term.	**· Spring Term.**	**Spring Term.**
Latin 4 (E)	Latin 4 (E)	Astronomy 3
Greek 4 (E)	Astronomy 3	Calculus B 3 E
Astronomy 3	Calculus B 3 (E)	Geology A 5
Calculus B 3 (E)	Geology A 5	Chemistry B 2-4
Geology A 5	Chemistry B 2-4	English Literature 5
Chemistry B 2-4 (E)	English Literature 5	Logic B 3 (E)
English Literature 5	Logic B 3 (E)	Bible and Rhetorical 2
Logic B 3 (E)	Bible and Rhetorical 2	(18 hours required.)
German 3	(18 hours required.)	
Bible and Rhetorical 2		
(18 hours required.)		
SENIOR YEAR.	**SENIOR YEAR.**	**SENIOR YEAR.**
Fall Term.	**Fall Term.**	**Fall Term.**
Porter's Intellect 5	Porter's Intellect 5	Porter's Intellect 5
Butler's Analogy 3 (E)	Economics 3	Economics 5
Economics 3	Constitution of U. S. 3	Constitution of U. S. 3
Constitution of U. S. 3	Geology B & C 5 (C E) (2	Geology B & C 5 (2 mos. ea.)
Geology B & C 5 (E) (2 mos.	mos. each).	Chemistry C 2-4
each).	Chemistry C 2-4 (E)	Anglo-Saxon or Eng. Lit. 2
Chemistry C 2-4 (E)	Trench on Words 2 (E)	(E)
Trench on Words 2	Anglo-Saxon or Eng. Lit. 2	Spanish 5 (E)
Anglo Saxon or Eng. Lit. 2	(E)	French 5 (E)
(E)	Spanish 5 (E)	Bible and Rhetorical 2
Spanish 5 (E)	French 5 (E)	
French 5 (E)	Bible and Rhetorical 2	
Bible and Rhetorical 2		
Spring Term.	**Spring Term.**	**Spring Term.**
Moral Science 3	Moral Science 3	Moral Science 3
Natural Theology 2 (E)	Natural Theology 2 (E)	Evidences of Christianity 3
History of Philosophy 3 (E)	History of Philosophy 3	International Law 3 (E)
Evidences of Christianity (3)	Evidences of Christianity 3	Guizot 3 (E)
International Law 3 (E)	International Law 3 (E)	Biology C 5 for 4 mos.
Guizot 3 (E)	Guizot 3 (E)	Anglo-Saxon or Eng. Lit. 2
Biology C 5 (E) for 4 mos.	Biology C 5 for 4 mos.	(E)
Anglo-Saxon or Eng. Lit. 2	Anglo-Saxon or Eng. Lit. 2	Spanish 5 (E)
(E)	(E)	French 5 (E)
Spanish 5 (E)	Spanish 5 (E)	Bible and Rhetorical 2
French 5 (E)	French 5 (E)	(18 hours required.),
Bible and Rhetorical 2	Bible and Rhetorical 2	
(18 hours required.)	(18 hours required.)	

Preparatory Department.

Classical Course.	Philosophical Course.	Scientific Course.
JUNIOR YEAR.	**JUNIOR YEAR.**	**JUNIOR YEAR.**
Fall Term.	**Fall Term.**	**Fall Term.**
First Latin 5 Arithmetic 5 Grammar; Word Study 4 Rhetoric 3 English Literature 1 Bible and Rhetorical 2	First Latin 5 Arithmetic 5 Grammar; Word Study 4 Rhetoric 3 English Literature 1 Bible and Rhetorical 2	U. S. History 5 Book-keeping 5 Arithmetic 5 Grammar; Word Study 4 Rhetoric 3 English Literature 1 Penmanship 5 Bible and Rhetorical 2
Spring Term.	**Spring Term.**	**Spring Term.**
First Latin 5 Algebra 4 Physical Geography 4 Rhetoric 4 Elocution 4 English Literature 1 Bible and Rhetorical 2	First Latin 5 Algebra 4 Physical Geography 4 Rhetoric 4 Elocution 4 English Literature 1 Bible and Rhetorical 2	Algebra 4 Physical Geography 4 Rhetoric 4 Book-keeping 3 Elocution 4 English Literature 1 Penmanship 5 Bible and Rhetorical 2
MIDDLE YEAR.	**MIDDLE YEAR.**	**MIDDLE YEAR.**
Fall Term.	**Fall Term.**	**Fall Term.**
Cæsar 5 Beginning Greek 5 Algebra 5 Physics 2 Word Study 5 English Literature 1 Bible and Rhetorical 2	Cæsar 5 German 4 Algebra 5 Physics 2 Word Study 5 English Literature 1 Bible and Rhetorical 2	German 4 Algebra 5 Physics 2 Word Study 5 English Literature 1 Bible and Rhetorical 2
Spring Term.	**Spring Term.**	**Spring Term.**
Cicero 5 Beginning Greek 5 Algebra 5 Physiology 3 Physics 2 Elocution 4 English Literature 1 Bible and Rhetorical 2	Cicero 5 German 4 Algebra 5 Physiology 3 Physics 2 Elocution 4 English Literature 1. Bible and Rhetorical 2	German 4 Algebra 5 Physics 2 Physiology 3 Elocution 4 English Literature 1 Bible and Rhetorical 2
SENIOR YEAR.	**SENIOR YEAR.**	**SENIOR YEAR.**
Fall Term.	**Fall Term.**	**Fall Term.**
Virgil 4 Anabasis 5 Algebra 5 General History 2 Bible and Eng. Literature 2	Virgil 4 German 5 Algebra 5 General History 2 Bible and Eng. Literature 2	German 5 Algebra 5 High School Arithmetic 5 General History 2 Bible and Eng. Literature 2
Spring Term.	**Spring Term.**	**Spring Term.**
Sallust 4 Iliad 5 Geometry 4 General History 4 Bible and Rhetorical 2	Sallust 4 German 5 Geometry 4 General History 4 Bible and Rhetorical 2	German 5 Geometry 4 High School Arithmetic 5 General History 4 Bible and Rhetorical 2

Teachers' Course.

FIRST YEAR.

Fall Term.

U. S. History 5
Arithmetic ; Intellectual
   Arithmetic 5
Geography 5
Grammar ; Word Study 5
American Literature 2
Penmanship 5
Bible and Rhetorical 2

Spring Term.

U. S. History 5
History of Tennessee 3
Arithmetic ; Intellectual
   Arithmetic 5
Geography 5
Grammar ; Word Study 5
Penmanship 5
Bible and Rhetorical 2

SECOND YEAR.

Fall Term.

First Latin 5
Higher Arithmetic 5
Grammar ; Word Study 4
Rhetoric 3
Book-keeping 3
English Literature 1
Bible and Rhetorical 2

Spring Term.

First Latin 5
Arithmetic 5
Algebra 5
Rhetoric 3
Book-keeping 3
English Literature 1
Bible and Rhetorical 2

THIRD YEAR.

Fall Term.

Cæsar 5
Algebra 5
Government of Tennessee 3
Pedagogy 3
Physics 2
English Literature 1
Bible and Rhetorical 2

Spring Term.

Cicero 5
Algebra 5
Physiology 3
Physics 2
Pedagogy 3
Elocution 4
English Literature 1
Bible and Rhetorical 2

FOURTH YEAR.

Fall Term.

Virgil 4
Higher Algebra 5
Geology of Tennessee 3
Elements of Agriculture 2
English Literature 1
Bible and Rhetorical 2

Spring Term.

Sallust 4
Geometry 5
General History 4
Civics 4
English Literature 1
Bible and Rhetorical 2

FIFTH YEAR.

Fall Term.

Trigonometry 5
Chemistry A 2-4
Physics A 4-2
Psychology 5
Rhetoric 2
Bible and Rhetorical 2

Spring Term.

Geometry 4
Geology 5
Pedagogy 3
English History 3
Rhetoric 3
Bible and Rhetorical 2

NOTE.—Graduates in this course of study, if they wish to pursue their studies further, will be admitted to the Sophomore Class of either the Classical or the Philosophical Course and to the Junior Class of the Scientific Course.

The Courses of Study.

The reception of the Fayerweather bequest has enabled the College to offer a greatly improved curriculum, and to arrange for the appointment of instructors to direct the many additional classes for which provision has been made in the revised curriculum. Many improvements will be noted by those who are familiar with the courses of study heretofore pursued, The provision for numerous electives in the Sophomore, Junior and Senior years ; the broadening of the Natural Science department ; the additional opportunities in the ancient and modern languages, mathematics, English literature, logic and rhetoric, and the establishment of a thorough course of study for a Teachers' Department, are the principal features of the most notable advance ever made in the long and honorable career of the institution.

Though the advance made involved the equalization of the three courses of study as to the number of years required to complete them, it is believed that the result in improved and more substantial scholarship will amply justify the elevation of the standard in those courses which have hitherto required fewer years for a degree than does the classical course. Those who still wish a shorter course may find it in the Teachers' Course, which is the equal of the most thorough offered in our State.

The general object of the courses of study is the thorough and symmetrical development of the intellectual powers and moral character of the student; not so much to make specialists as to graduate men fully equipped for the highest demands that may be made of college-bred men everywhere. The liberally educated man is best equipped for achieving success in any special work to which he may be called in subsequent life.

The electives are confined to those years when the student has probably discovered his special aptitudes, and has attained to that degree of culture which will make it safe for him to select some of his studies.

Philosophy, and Economic and Political Science.

PRESIDENT BOARDMAN.

The best text-books are employed, with books of reference in all the departments, so far as accessible. These are used with free and independent discussion of all topics involved in the branches pursued.

23

Ancient Languages and Literature.

Latin.

PROF. NEWMAN AND AN ASSISTANT INSTRUCTOR.

PREPARATORY. JUNIOR YEAR, FALL TERM: *Five hours a week.* —First Book in Latin.

SPRING TERM: *Five hours a week.*—First Book in Latin completed; Collar's Gate to Cæsar; Prose Composition; simple exercises in sight reading.

MIDDLE YEAR, FALL TERM: *Five hours a week.*—Gate to Cæsar for four weeks, with exercises in sight reading and a review of declensions and conjugations; Cæsar, Books i, iii, and iv, with a study of the subjunctive mode and the subject of indirect discourse.

SPRING TERM: *Five hours a week.*—Cicero, Orations i, ii and iii, with written parsing and special study of the subjunctive mode; prose composition, part iii.

SENIOR YEAR, FALL TERM: *Four hours a week.*—Virgil's Æneid, Books i, ii and iii; special attention to Mythology and scansion in dactylic hexameter.

SPRING TERM: *Four hours a week.*—Sallust's Jugurtha or Catiline; thorough review of grammar; Prose Composition; special work in the subjunctive mode; practice in sight reading.

Harkness' Grammar is used in all preparatory classes. The Roman method of pronunciation is employed. The object aimed at in all this preparatory work is ease and accuracy in translation, and hence stress is laid upon (1) the acquisition of a vocabulary, (2) the mastery of inflections, and (3) the uses of the subjunctive mode.

COLLEGE FRESHMAN YEAR, FALL TERM: *Four hours a week.*— Livy, Book xxi, with sight reading from Book i; outlines in grammar.

SPRING TERM: *Four hours a week.*—Cicero de Senectute et Amicitia; Prose Composition; Myers' Roman History.

SOPHOMORE YEAR, FALL TERM: *Four hours a week.*—Pliny the Younger, selections from his letters showing the life of a Roman as an advocate, provincial governor, gentleman and man of letters in the Empire: this for eight weeks; Horace, Odes and Ars Poetica, with special attention to the meters of the poet.—*Elective in Classical and required in Philosophical.*

SPRING TERM: *Four hours a week.*—Tacitus, Agricola, with sketch of Britain as a Roman province, and also a review of the conditions of the Empire from Nero to Trajan; Seneca, Moral Essays; Prose Composition.—*Elective in Classical and required in Philosophical.*

JUNIOR YEAR, FALL TERM: *Four hours a week.*—Plautus, Menæchmi and Captivi, with a study of the development of the Latin comedy, the antiquities of the stage and the introduction to Latin as a spoken language.—*Elective.*

SPRING TERM : *Four hours a week.*—Latin Literature ; selections from various authors illustrating the development of the language ; lectures by the professor in charge ; essays by the students upon special subjects connected with the term's work.—*Elective.*

In all college classes, Allen and Greenough's Grammar is used.

Students wishing to enter any class in the Latin course will be examined in the studies of the previous year or an equivalent.

Greek.

PROF. SHERRILL AND AN ASSISTANT INSTRUCTOR.

PREPARATORY. MIDDLE YEAR, FALL TERM : *Five hours a week.*—White's Beginner's Greek Book.

SPRING TERM : *Five hours a week.*—White's Beginner's Greek Book ; Anabasis begun.

Special study of Syntax, and forms and properties of words.

SENIOR YEAR, FALL TERM : *Five hours a week.*—Goodwin's Anabasis, two books ; Myers' History of Greece ; Geography of Ancient Greece and Asia Minor.

SPRING TERM : *Five hours a week.*—Homer's Iliad ; Mythology ; Geography.

During this year special stress is placed on the study of grammatical constructions, idioms and dialectic forms. Exercises are had in sight reading. Thorough study of the grammar is made, in connection with the text.

COLLEGE. FRESHMAN YEAR, FALL TERM : *Four hours a week.*—Mather's Selections from Herodotus, Prose Composition.

SPRING TERM : *Four hours a week.*—Thucydides, book vii ; Prose Composition.

During this year the characteristics of the authors are pointed out, and a careful study of the text, of syntax and of word formation is combined with practice in translation at sight.

SOPHOMORE YEAR, FALL TERM : *Four hours a week.*—Plato's Protagoras ; Æschylus' Seven against Thebes ; Prose Composition.—*Elective.*

SPRING TERM : *Four hours a week.*—Demosthenes ; History of Greek Literature.—*Elective.*

In the authors read in the Sophomore year, the thought and the style receive special consideration. In the second term a careful study is made of Jebb's History of Greek Literature.

In the prescribed work of the Freshman and Sophomore years, the courses are arranged with a view to acquiring a facility in reading the easier authors at sight, and to acquiring some knowledge of the most striking features of the private life of the Greeks, and of an outline history of their literature.

JUNIOR YEAR, FALL TERM: *Four hours a week.*—Andocides' De Mysteriis.—*Elective.*

SPRING TERM: *Four hours a week.*—Aristophanes' Plutus.—*Elective.*

Mathematics.

PROF. WALLER.

For the earlier preparatory mathematics see the synopsis of the preparatory curriculum. Prof. Waller's classes are as follows:

PREPARATORY. SENIOR YEAR, FALL TERM: *Five hours a week.*—Wentworth's Complete Algebra; involution and evolution, quadratic equations, inequalities, radical expressions and logarithms.

SPRING TERM: *Four hours a week.*—Wentworth's Plane Geometry, the first three books, with the original exercises.

COLLEGE. FRESHMAN YEAR, FALL TERM: *Four hours a week.*—Wentworth's Complete Algebra, proportion; series, choice, binomial and exponential theorems, indeterminate co-efficients, the differential method and equations in general.

SPRING TERM: *Four hours a week.*—Wentworth's Geometry: Books iv and v of Plane Geometry and all of Solid Geometry; numerous exercises and original propositions are also required.

SOPHOMORE YEAR, FALL TERM: *Four hours a week.*—Wentworth's Plane Trigonometry and Surveying; enough field work is given in surveying to illustrate the principles of compass surveying.

SPRING TERM: *Four hours a week, for one month.*—Spherical Trigonometry. Also, as an *elective, four hours a week;* Plane Analytical Geometry; this course includes the study of the subject as given in the first seven chapters of Wentworth's Analytical Geometry, omitting the supplementary propositions.

JUNIOR YEAR, FALL TERM: *Four hours a week.*—Elements of Differential and integral Calculus; this course includes what is given in Taylor's Elements of Calculus as far as the evaluation of the Maxima and Minima.—*Elective.*

SPRING TERM: *Three hours a week.*—Calculus: this course is a continuation of the preceding course.—*Elective.* Astronomy: *Three hours a week.*—The subject as presented in Young's General Astronomy is made the basis of work, taking the more important topics.

The Natural Sciences.

PROF. FISHER AND AN ASSISTANT INSTRUCTOR.

Chemistry.

JUNIOR YEAR, FALL TERM: *Six hours a week.*—A. General Inorganic Chemistry; recitations, lecture-table experiments by the Professor, and laboratory work by the student.

SPRING TERM: *Six hours a week.*—B. Qualitative and Quantitative Analysis; lectures and laboratory work.

SENIOR YEAR, FALL TERM: *Six hours a week.*—C. Organic Chemistry, Theoretic and Practical; recitations and laboratory work.

In course A, the elements of inorganic chemistry are taught by recitations, by lectures, and by laboratory work which the student is required to perform for himself, in this manner illustrating the principles set forth in the text-book.

Course B is devoted entirely to chemical analysis by both the wet and dry way. Both gravimetric and volumetric methods will be used. Almost the entire work of this course will be done in the laboratory by the student.

Course C consists of elementary organic chemistry: in this division it is intended to supplement the text by laboratory work, and thus render practical to the student so much of the subject as the class may be able to cover.

Physics.

SOPHOMORE YEAR, FALL TERM: *Six hours a week.*—A. The Elements of Physics, with experiments; recitations from the text-book; lecture-table experiments by the Professor; laboratory practice by the student.

SPRING TERM: *Five hours a week.*—B. Laboratory practice in physical measurements. Course A must have preceded this course.

JUNIOR YEAR, FALL TERM: *Four hours a week.*—C. Electricity and Magnetism, advanced work, with laboratory practice.

Course A is intended to furnish the student with a clear idea of the principles of elementary physics, and to afford him the opportunity to demonstrate by practical work at the laboratory table as many of these principles as the time will permit.

Course B consists almost exclusively in practice in phyical measurements by the student at the laboratory table. To test the student's knowledge of the work done a series of carefully graded exercises will be given by the teacher.

Course C is intended to make the student familiar with practical work in the modern applications of electricity and magnetism.

The Biological Sciences.

FRESHMAN YEAR, Fall Term: *Five hours a week.*—The Elements of Botany and Zoölogy.

Spring Term: *Five hours a week.*—Botany and Zoölogy advanced, chiefly microscopic work.

SENIOR YEAR, Spring Term: *Five hours a week.*—C. Human Physiology advanced, with the science of health as it relates to the prevention of disease, exercise, food, etc.

Course A is intended to give the student a knowledge of the elements of botany and zoölogy, and to enable him to classify plants and animals. The work consists of recitations from the text, demonstrations by the professor, and the use of the microscope by the student.

Course B consists of microscopic work in the laboratory; of a study of plant and animal tissues, and the development of the plant and animal.

Course C is intended to afford the student a good knowledge of the structure and functions of the human body, and to afford an introduction to the study of medicine. Course C should be taken only after a careful study of some elementary work on physiology and of courses A and B, together with physics and chemistry.

Geology.

JUNIOR YEAR, Spring Term: *Five hours a week.*—A. The Elements of Geology.

SENIOR YEAR, Fall Term: *Five hours a week for two months.*—B. Advanced Physical Geography. *Five hours a week.*—C. Meteorology, Theoretical and Practical.

Course A will cover the subjects of dynamical, structural and historical geology, and will afford the student a good knowledge of the elements of geology.

Courses B and C are supplementary to course A, and are intended to show the student something of the physical geography and meteorological conditions of the past, and their relation to geology.

So far as time permits, course C will consist of the practical study of the weather conditions, and the methods of making forecasts as now practiced by the weather bureau.

In all courses text-books will be used, and the work supplemented by lectures by the teacher.

Course A of each branch of Natural Science will be required of all three courses of study, the classical, the philosophical and the scientific; course B will be required of the philosophical and scientific courses, and will be elective to those of the classical course who have completed course A; course C will be required of the scientific course, and will be elective to those of the other courses who have completed courses A and B. The figures 2–4 in the Synopsis mean two hours of recitation and four hours of the laboratory work.

English Language and Literature.

PROF. WILSON AND AN ASSISTANT INSTRUCTOR.

PREPARATORY. JUNIOR YEAR, FALL TERM : *One hour a week.* —Read Ivanhoe ; study Burke's Speech on Conciliation with America.

SPRING TERM : *One hour a week.*—Read The Last of the Mohicans ; study Merchant of Venice.

MIDDLE YEAR, FALL TERM : *One hour a week.*—Read Silas Marner and Pope's Iliad, books i, vi, xxii and xxiv.

SPRING TERM : *One hour a week.*—Read The House of Seven Ga. bles ; Sir Roger de Coverley ; study L'Allegro and Il Penseroso ; study Macaulay on Milton and Addison.

SENIOR YEAR, FALL TERM : *One hour a week.*—Read The Princess, and The Ancient Mariner ; study Macbeth.

The above schedule of study and reading comprises one of the courses suggested by the Conference on Uniform Entrance Requirements in English. The effort will be made, by means of this attractive course of reading and study, to cultivate a taste for literature which shall lead the students voluntarily to avail themselves of the advantages afforded them by the library, and to read with discriminating appreciation many more than the required books.

COLLEGE. FRESHMAN YEAR, SPRING TERM : *Three hours a week.*—Montgomery's History of England will be required in all the courses, to provide the necessary basis for an intelligent study, first, of the English language, and then, of the English literature.

SOPHOMORE YEAR, FALL TERM : *One hour a week.*—Lounsbury's History of the English Language. The development of our language, and its special fitness as a vehicle of the best thought of the ages, will be discussed in recitations and lectures.

Two hours a week, for two months.—A review in syntactic analysis of English sentences is taken, with Bunyan's Pilgrim's Progress as a text. The sentences are analyzed by pointing out all the combinations made, whether predicative, objective, adverbial or attributive. The work is done in the way illustrated in Dr. March's Method of the Philological Study of the English Language. In no way can the mechanics of the English sentence be mastered more speedily or thoroughly.

Two hours a week, for two months.—Outlining or analysis of topics for discussion. This practical work is done in accordance with a system of principles and rules collated by the professor in charge. The absolute necessity of method in all composition is so emphasized by this course, that it is believed that, after the two months' drill, few if any of the students who have taken it ever begin any work in composition without first framing an outline of the proposed work. Ten outlines of assigned topics are presented by each student, and criticised and returned by the professor.

SPRING TERM : *Three hours a week.*—Genung's Practical Elements of Rhetoric, with illustrative examples, is studied, and the students are familiarized with the principles of style and invention, and a few practical exercises accompany the study of the text-book.

Three hours a week.—Studies in the English and American literature of the Nineteenth Century. By the reading and criticism of extracts from the works of a goodly number of the leading authors of the century, the way will be prepared for the more general survey of literature to be taken in the Junior Year.—*Elective.*

· JUNIOR YEAR, FALL TERM : *Four hours a week.*—Shakespeare's Julius Cæsar and Hamlet, studied principally as master-pieces of dramatic art ; Milton's Paradise Lost, with study of the first book word by word, and then the reading and discussion of the entire poem. Sprague's Paradise Lost is used by the class. Four hours for two months is devoted to Shakespeare and the same to Milton. Either Shakespeare or Milton is required ; the other is elective.

Three hours a week.—Course B in Rhetoric. This course consists of the practical application of the principles enunciated in Course A, and is elective for those who have passed in Course A. The work will be altogether practical, and will consist of rhetorical criticism of passages of English prose literature and of sentences, paragraphs and longer compositions prepared by the student, either in or for the recitation room.

Five hours a week.—Hill's Jevons' Logic, studied in connection with printed questions and exercises prepared for the class. All the practical work given in the exercises appended in the text-book will be required, and original work will be introduced. Logic in its relations to composition and literature will be discussed.

JUNIOR YEAR, SPRING TERM : *Five hours a week.*—A survey of the entire field of English literature. As a guide Maclean's Chart is employed, but most of the time is devoted to the reading and criticism of specimens from the works of forty or more authors, from Chaucer's time to the present. As a review, a rapid reading of some approved compendium is required.

Three hours a week.—Logic, Course B. This course, elective for those who have passed in Course A, is entirely confined to practical work in Deduction and Inductive Logic. The object aimed at will be the conscious and speedy application of the laws of Logic to the argumentative reasoning of ourselves and others.

SENIOR YEAR, FALL TERM : *Two hours a week.*—Trench's Study of Words, with the addition of lists of words for etymological study.

Two hours a week.—Anglo Saxon, Grammar and Reader.—*Elective.*

Two hours a week.—English Literature ; History and Fiction. These subjects will be studied topically, and oral and written reports will be presented by the class.—*Elective.*

SPRING TERM.—English style. Each. Senior will do literary work under the direction of the instructor, but there will be no stated recitations and no class work. The individual style of each Senior will be considered and criticised. The equivalent of two hours a week will be required.

Two hours a week.—Anglo-Saxon, Grammar and Reader.—*Elective.*

History.

Montgomery's American History and Phelan's History of Tennessee are provided for in both terms of the earlier preparatory years, and in the first years of the Teachers' Course.

PROFS. GILL and ELLIS and MISS HENRY.

PREPARATORY. SENIOR YEAR, FALL TERM : *Five hours a week for five weeks.*—Myers' History of Greece.   PROF. SHERRILL.

Two hours a week.—Myers' General History, studied with the help of printed summaries and questions prepared by the professor in charge.
PROF. WILSON.

SPRING TERM : *Four hours a week.*—Myers' General History, concluded.   PROF. WILSON.

COLLEGE. FRESHMAN YEAR, SPRING TERM : *Three hours a week.*—Montgomery's History of England, with frequent drill and review with the help of printed topics and questions prepared by the professor in charge.   PROF. WILSON.

Four hours a week, for six weeks.—Myers' History of Rome.
PROF. NEWMAN.

SENIOR YEAR, SPRING TERM : *Three hours a week.*—Guizot's History of Civilization in Europe, studied with the help of a printed synopsis prepared by the professor in charge.—*Elective.*   PROF. WILSON.

Besides the above-mentioned courses in pure history, courses in the History of the English Language, the History of English Literature and the History of Philosophy are given. The object aimed at in the department of History is the mastery of the outline facts found in an approved text-book on the subject studied, and the cultivation of an interest in the career of mankind as a race, and an intelligent appreciation of the philosophy of history. The ordinary class-room work will be supplemented by occasional lectures by the instructors.

The Modern Languages.

MISS ANDREWS, FRENCH AND GERMAN; PROF. WILSON, SPANISH.

German.

PREPARATORY. MIDDLE YEAR, FALL TERM: *Four hours a week.* The term is devoted mainly to drill in pronunciation, the common forms of inflection, sentence structure, and the use of the German script. Whitney's Brief German Grammar and Worman's First German Book are the text-books used.

SPRING TERM: *Four hours a week.*—Two hours a week are devoted to composition and conversation drill based upon Collar's Eysenbach German Lessons, and two hours a week to easy reading from Whitney's Introductory German Reader. Beginning with this term the recitations are conducted mainly in the German language.

SENIOR YEAR, FALL TERM: *Five hours a week.*—Two hours a week are devoted to composition and conversation drill, based upon Collar's Eysenbach, and three hours to reading. Whitney's Reader is completed this term.

SPRING TERM: *Five hours a week.*—Two hours a week are devoted to composition and conversation drill, and three hours to reading Schiller's Jungfrau von Orleans and Gœthe's Hermann and Dorothea.

COLLEGE. FRESHMAN YEAR, FALL TERM: *Four hours a week.*— Composition and conversation, one hour a week. Reading Schiller's William Tell and Gœthe's Egmont, three hours a week.

SPRING TERM: *Four hours a week.*—Composition and conversation, one hour a week. Reading Dippold's Scientific German Reader and Scheffel's Ekkehard, three hours a week.

The above three years' course is required in the Philosophical and Scientific Courses.

SOPHOMORE YEAR, BOTH TERMS: *Three hours a week.*—Joynes-Meissner German Grammar and Joynes' German Reader, and Storme's Immensee. Daily drill in sentence structure and the use of the script is given.

JUNIOR YEAR, FALL TERM: *Three hours a week.*—Schiller's William Tell.

SPRING TERM: *Three hours a week.*—Gœthe's Egmont and Lessing's Nathan der Weise, with sight reading from easy German comedies.

The above Sophomore and Junior work is required of the Classical Course students.

French.

SENIOR YEAR, FALL TERM: *Five hours a week.*—Chardenal's Complete French Course, First Part, and Worman's First French Book. —*Elective* in all the courses.

SPRING TERM : *Five hours a week.*—Chardenal's Complete French Course, Second Part, and Moliere's L'Avarre, or some other French comedy.—*Elective* in all the courses.

Spanish.

SENIOR YEAR, FALL TERM : *Five hours a week.*—De Tornos' Combined Spanish Method is used. Beginning with the second lesson the principal exercises are the translation of English into Spanish and of Spanish into English, as the sentences are read by the student. The object is to enable the student to speak fluently enough by the close of the year to be equipped for successful work in Spanish-speaking countries, so far as a fair knowledge of a language can equip one for success.

SPRING TERM : *Five hours a week.*—De Tornos' Combined Method completed in four weeks ; Zarate's Compendio de Historia General de Mejico, read for two months ; El Principe Constante de Calderon de la Barca, read in two months.—*Both terms elective* in all the courses.

Department of Music.

MISS PERINE.

The work in this department is continually advancing. A pleasant room in Anderson Hall has been fitted up by the college for the music-room, and an expensive and rich-toned piano placed in it. There are also pianos in Baldwin Hall and the college practice-room, and all students who desire may secure ample practice hours at very reasonable rates.

Classes in Theory of Music are organized at the beginning of each term, thus giving opportunity for study in this important branch of musical knowledge.

A costly and handsome organ has been placed in the chapel, and those desiring may receive instruction upon this instrument.

In connection with the piano lessons special attention is given to sight-reading and *ensemble* playing.

At the piano and organ, instruction is given privately in half-hour lessons.

Preparatory Department.

PROF. BARNES, PRINCIPAL.

This department is designed to prepare students for the regular course of the college. It also provides facilities for a large and worthy class of young people who have a limited amount of means and time at their command to acquire some preparation for their future work. Classes are formed each term in common branches, Algebra, Geometry, Latin, Greek and German, if even only a small number of students desire to take these studies. This is done for the especial benefit of teachers and irregular students.

Candidates for admission to this department must furnish satisfactory evidence of good moral character, and must pass examination in Geography, Arithmetic as far as percentage, English Grammar as far as syntax. Students over fifteen years of age who have not had the advantage of early training, and who fail to pass the entrance examination, are prepared for entrance in a room provided for that purpose ; but pupils under fifteen years of age who fail to pass the entrance examination are not permitted to enter the department.

The department is under the special supervision of Professor Barnes, the Principal. The classes are taught by the regular professors, instructors, tutors and teachers. Four parallel courses, corresponding to the college courses, are offered.

Teachers' Department.

This course is designed to equip intending teachers thoroughly for their profession, and to afford those who are already members of the profession opportunities for further study. A five years' course is offered. It is arranged to prepare teachers especially for the Primary and Secondary schools of Tennessee. As in the other departments of the college, the classes are conducted by the regular professors, who are specialists. In addition to the work done in the other departments, this department requires the following courses which are taught by Prof. Barnes :

PEDAGOGY. I. Theory and Practice. This course is designed to inculate such practical views as will best promote the improvement of the young teacher, and will enable him to teach successfully in the common school. Page's Theory and Practice is used as a text-book.

II. Elements of Psychology and Pedagogy. The aim of the course is to teach the elements of psychology in order to enable the student to learn and to apply the fundamental principles of teaching. White's Pedagogy and Compayre's Psychology Applied to Education are used as text-books.

III. The aim of this course is to give the student a comprehensive, clear and accurate knowledge of the Theory and Practice of Education. The text-book used is Compayre's Lectures on Pedagogy.

PSYCHOLOGY. This course is designed to teach both the Elements and Principles of Psychology, and to prepare the student for Course III in Pedagogy. It includes the subjects of habit, will, instinct, attention,

The Walk View.

elaboration, sensation and the nervous mechanism. Mental facts are treated, as far as possible, from an experimental and analytical point of view. James' Psychology, Briefer Course, and Hoffding's Outlines of Psychology will be used in alternate years.

CIVICS. I. This course includes a careful study of the History of the Constitution of Tennessee, and of the present government of the State. The text-book is Karns' Government of Tennessee.

II. History of the Constitution, including a careful analysis of the same, is given in this course. It also includes a study of local, county and State government. McCleary's text is used.

Maryville College.

History.

Maryville College was founded in 1819. It was born of the moral and spiritual needs of the earliest settlers of East Tennessee—chiefly Scotch-Irish Presbyterians— and was designed to educate for the ministry men who should be native to the soil. The grand motive of the founder may be stated in his own words : " LET THE DIRECTORS AND MANAGERS OF THIS SACRED INSTITUTION PROPOSE THE GLORY OF GOD AND THE ADVANCEMENT OF THAT KINGDOM PURCHASED BY THE BLOOD OF HIS ONLY BEGOTTEN SON, AS THEIR SOLE OBJECT." Inspired by such a motive, Rev. Isaac Anderson, D.D., gathered a class of five in the fall of 1819, and in prayer and faith began the work of his life. In forty-two ·years the institution put one hundred and fifty men into the ministry. Its endowment, gathered by littles through all these years, was only sixteen thousand dollars.

Then came the Civil War, and suspended the work of the institution for five years, and the College came out of the general wreck with little save its good name and precious history.

After the war, the Synod of Tennessee, moved by the spirit of self-preservation and by a desire to promote Christian education in the Central South, resolved to revive Maryville College. The institution was reopened in 1866. New grounds and new buildings were an imperative necessity. To meet this need, sixty-five thousand dollars were secured, and the College was saved from extinction. In 1881, a few generous friends contributed an endowment fund of one hundred thousand dollars. Seven years ago Daniel Fayerweather bequeathed to the College the sum of one hundred thousand dollars. The College was also made one of twenty equal participants in the residuary estate, and has received almost all of the two hundred and fifty thousand dollars to which it is entitled by the provisions of the will. This magnificent donation has enabled the institution to enlarge its work and to enter upon a new era of usefulness and influence. About seventy of the post-bellum Alumni have entered the ministry, while nineteen Alumni and undergraduates have been or are missionaries in Japan, China, Corea, India, Persia, Syria, Africa and Mexico. Several are laboring in missions on the Western frontier. All the Alumni are engaged in honorable pursuits. Students who have gone from the College to the theological, medical and legal schools, have usually attained a high rank in their

The President's Residence.

The Lamar Library.

classes. A goodly number of the Alumni are now studying in theological seminaries.

The necessary expenses are so phenomenally low as to give the institution a special adaptation to the middle class and to the struggling poor—the great mass of the surrounding population.

The privileges of the institution are open alike to all denominations of Christians.

Location.

Maryville is a pleasant and thriving town of about two thousand five hundred inhabitants. There is no saloon in Blount county. Maryville is widely known as " the town of schools and churches." It is the present terminus of the Knoxville and Augusta Railroad, and is sixteen miles distant from Knoxville. There are two trains a day, each way, on the K. and A. Railroad. Knoxville is approached from the South and West via Chattanooga, or Dalton, or Marietta; from the North and Northwest via Junction City (Danville) and Jellico, or via Harriman Junction, or via Cumberland Gap; from the Southeast via Asheville: from the Northeast via Lynchburg and Bristol. A hack line also connects with Chandler's, a station on the Atlanta, Knoxville and Northern Railroad, six miles distant from Maryville.

Grounds and Buildings.

The College grounds consist of two hundred and fifty acres, and for beautiful scenery are not surpassed by any in the country. They are elevated and undulating, covered with a beautiful growth of evergreens and with a noble forest, and command a splendid view of the Cumberland mountains on the north, and of the Smoky mountains on the south.

The location is as remarkable for its healthfulness as it is for its beauty. The *campus* affords the choicest facilities for the development of athletics.

On these grounds there are nine buildings, which were erected at a cost of about one hundred thousand dollars.

The central building is adapted to college purposes and is used exclusively for them. In honor of the founder of the institution it is called ANDERSON HALL. The large addition to the Hall, THE FAYERWEATHER ANNEX, forty by ninety feet in size, is occupied by the Preparatory Department, and has added greatly to its success. BALDWIN HALL, named in honor of the late John C. Baldwin, of New Jersey, is occupied by the young ladies. In this Hall accommodations for board are provided by the Coöperative Boarding Club for all the members of the institution who choose to board there. Three years ago an Annex was added to this Hall. The size of the new building is forty by seventy-five feet, with a dining-room large enough for two hundred boarders, and with rooms on the second and third floors for occupancy by the young ladies. MEMORIAL HALL is occupied by the young men. These Halls are large and convenient, well lighted and ventilated, and will accommodate one hundred and thirty students. The College buildings are connected with the electric system of the town. The College also owns two PROFESSORS' HOUSES and the JANITOR'S HOUSE. THE LAMAR MEMORIAL LIBRARY building is spoken of on another page. THE PRESIDENT'S RESIDENCE was provided in 1890 by a magnificent gift of Mrs. Jane F. Willard. It adorns College Hill and is a valuable property. It bears the following inscription :

PRESIDENT'S HOUSE,

ERECTED AS A MEMORIAL OF HER HUSBAND,

SYLVESTER WILLARD, M.D.,

BY

MRS. JANE F. WILLARD,

1890.

The new Y. M. C. A. and Gymnasium building, BARTLETT HALL, and the new SCIENCE BUILDING are spoken of elsewhere.

Work has been begun on the extensive system of walks and drives that has recently been surveyed and mapped out by a competent civil engineer. It is expected that before many years the grounds, so beautiful by nature, will be rendered doubly attractive by art.

The New Science Building.

FAYERWEATHER SCIENCE HALL, erected in the summer of 1898, is one of the handsomest buildings on College Hill. The building is of brick, two stories high, with a basement 35x40 under the rear. The extreme dimensions are 106x97 feet. The trimmings are of marble and buff brick.

The first floor will be devoted chiefly to laboratory purposes ; there are six laboratories on this floor, one for each of the three divisions of work in chemistry, and the same number for laboratory work in physics ; in addition to the laboratories there is a balance room for exact weighing and storage rooms for both physical and chemical apparatus. The entrance is through a handsome balcony into a commodious hall into which all apartments open.

The second floor contains excellent class rooms. This floor also contains a laboratory for botany, one for zoölogy, a musuem, an office, storage rooms for biological and physical apparatus, and a fine hall through which access is had to the various rooms and to the upper balcony.

With the exception of the laboratory of organic chemistry and the balance room, all apartments measure from 25x30 to 25x40 feet in the

Fagerweather Science Hall.

clear. All are well-lighted and ventilated, and will be heated with steam and furnished with gas.

The upper front balcony affords not only a good view of the other college buildings and the grounds, but also a fine exposure for instruments for the practical study of meteorology.

The building is large, handsome and well-arranged; it will be provided with a liberal equipment for the practical study of the natural sciences, and will stand a useful and lasting monument to the prince of givers, Daniel B. Fayerweather.

Admission to the College.

Candidates for admission to the Freshman Class who have taken their preparatory course elsewhere, will be examined in the studies pursued by the Senior Class of the Preparatory Department of this College, or in their equivalents, unless they bring certificates that will be satisfactory to the Faculty; but a student thus receiving credit for a study pursued elsewhere will be conditioned until his subsequent work in the College proves his efficiency in the study thus accredited.

Candidates for admission to the Sophomore, Junior and Senior Classes are examined in the studies that have been pursued by the class which they wish to enter, or in others equivalent.

Those bringing certificates of dismission from another college may, upon proof of their qualifications satisfactory to the Faculty, be admitted to a corresponding standing in this College.

Those students who are absent from their classes for a part of the year must sustain a satisfactory examination in the studies pursued by the class during their absence, before they can reënter it.

Students who desire to pursue only a part of the studies of any course laid down in this catalogue, may be allowed to do so in connection with the regular classes, by special permission of the Faculty. Candidates for admission, and students who in any examination receive conditions, will be required to cancel them within the time designated by the Faculty. No student will be allowed to discontinue a study, except as he secures permission from the Faculty to do so.

Every student who offers himself for admission must present a testimonial of good character from some responsible person.

Students from other institutions cannot be admitted into this College unless honorably dismissed by their former instructor.

No student under fifteen years of age will be admitted to the Preparatory Department, unless qualified to enter the Junior year of the Classical Preparatory Course.

Absence from the College.

It is very important that students should be present at the beginning of each term, and continue to the end of it. Only in cases of extreme necessity should a student leave his studies just before the close of the collegiate year.

Administrative Rules.

Prayers are attended in the College Chapel in the morning, with the reading of the Scriptures and with singing; and the students are required to attend public worship on the Sabbath, and to connect themselves with a Bible Class in some one of the churches in town.

The use of tobacco on the College grounds and in the College buildings is forbidden, and no student addicted to its use will be allowed to room upon the College premises. One violation of this rule will be deemed sufficient to exclude a student from Memorial Hall.

All unexcused delinquencies are registered ; and when the number amounts to fifteen, notice thereof is given to the student, and to his parents or guardian. When the sum of unexcused delinquencies and demerits amount to twenty-five, the student ceases to be a member of the College. A delinquency is a failure to perform any College duty.

Students are also dismissed whenever, in the opinion of the Faculty, they are pursuing a course of conduct detrimental to themselves and to the College.

Students are not permitted to room or to board in places disapproved by the Faculty.

Students are not allowed to absent themselves from the College without permission from the Faculty.

Students are not permitted to engage in dramatic entertainments, and must secure special permission before engaging in any entertainment outside the College.

Students are not allowed to patronize the Sunday train. No student will be received on the Sabbath.

A student absent from any monthly examination without an approved excuse will be marked " zero " on that examination.

Any student failing to be present at term examination shall be required to take all examinations omitted, before being permitted to enter classes in any department upon his return to College.

A special examination will be granted to any student who desires credit for any required study which he has not taken in regular classroom work of this Institution.

Recording of Grades.

A uniform system of grading is employed, upon the results of which depends the promotion from one class to another.

The Faculty meet every week of the College year, and receive reports of the work done in all departments and of the delinquencies of individual students. Every month a record is made of the standing of each student, which is sent to his parents or guardian at the end of each quarter.

Degrees.

The degree of BACHELOR OF ARTS is conferred upon all graduates of the Classical Course.

The Degree of BACHELOR OF PHILOSOPHY will be conferred upon those who have completed the Philosophical Course.

The Degree of BACHELOR OF SCIENCE will be conferred on graduates of the Scientific Course.

Students who do not take a regular course may, upon a satisfactory examination, be granted a certificate with regard to their proficiency in the studies they have pursued.

At their last annual meeting, the Board of Directors adopted the following rule as to the degree of A.M. :

That the degree of A.M. in course be hereafter conferred after three years of Academic, Collegiate, Theological Seminary or University post-graduate work ; the presentation of a Thesis upon a topic assigned by the Faculty ; the Thesis to be approved by the Faculty ; and, finally, the payment of five dollars for the diploma.

The following degrees were conferred at the annual commencement, May 26, 1898 : A.B. : John Edmund Biddle, Fay Vilerie Caldwell, Frederick Starr Campbell, Wilson A. Eisenhart, Horace Lee Ellis, Carl Hopkins Elmore, Pliny Brokaw Ferris, Samuel Albert Harris, Samuel O'Grady Houston, Thomas Bartholomew Lillard, John Woodside Ritchie, Elmer Bruce Smith. B.L. : Marguerite Caldwell, Helen Ianthe Minnis, Cordelia Josephine Young. B.S. : Reuben Powel.

Religious Exercises.

The College is preëminently a religious institution. All its instructors are in the deepest sympathy with the doctrine that the culture of the soul is of the first importance. The history of the past has been one of gracious revivals. It has become a time-honored custom to devote ten days every February to a series of services in which the claims of God upon the young are forcibly presented by some approved minister. The lessons assigned are abridged during the continuance of the services. So greatly have these meetings been blessed that the College year closes with almost all the students numbered as professing Christians. Besides the daily worship conducted in the chapel, religious services are held every Tuesday evening, at which usually a professor of the College presides. The Y. M. C. A. and Y. W. C. A., established and conducted by the students, exert a most salutary influence upon the entire College. The Y. M. C. A. meets at present in the Chapel. The Y. W. C. A. meets in the parlors at BALDWIN HALL. The past year has been one of prosperity in the history of these Associations. The officers of the Y. M. C. A. are : President, Thomas Maguire ; Vice-President, T. H. McConnell ; Recording Secretary, I. W. Jones ; Corresponding Secretary, C. N. Magill ; Treasurer, H. C. Rimmer. The officers of the Y. W. C. A. are ; President, Miss Ethel B. Minnis ; Vice-President, Miss Edith L. Newman ; Recording Secretary, Miss Ora Rankin ; Treasurer, Miss Emma Alexander. The building for the Y. M. C. A. is not yet completed. As soon as money can be secured, the rooms to be used by the Association will be finished and put into immediate use.

Bible Study.

Systematic study of the English Bible is part of the permanent College curriculum. All the professors and instructors have weekly classes for the study of the Scriptures. The interest in the classes is deepening every year. Every part of the Word of God is brought under careful examination. The text-book employed has been Steele's Outlines of Bible Study. A generous gift of the Misses Willard—$200, to be expended in providing text-books and other aids for Bible Study—has been of great assistance in developing this department of study. In the Junior year of the Classical Course the Bible study is devoted to the New Testament in Greek.

Rhetorical Drill.

All students of the College, meeting in different classes, participate in the weekly rhetorical exercises. One essay and one declamation each month are required of all. By means of text-books and class-room work students are given an opportunity to acquire a scientific knowledge of the principles of vocal expression. Practice is given to exercises that promote voice power, clear articulation, correct modulation, and compass and purity of tone.

The Lamar Memorial Library.

The Lamar Memorial Library Hall was erected in 1888 at a cost of five thousand five hundred dollars, which amount was generously provided by three friends of Professor Lamar and of the College. The building is a model in every respect. It is a noble and fitting monument. The large memorial window contributed by the brothers and sisters of Professor Lamar holds the central position.

The Library itself is now one of the largest in Tennessee. This year has been notable for the large additions of books, through purchase or generous gifts. The entire number of books now on the shelves is over eleven thousand. The Library is open for the drawing of books or for consulting the volumes in the reference alcove for six hours every day from Monday to Friday, and for three hours on Saturdays. The advantages of the Library are entirely free to the students of all the courses. The results of the use of the Library are manifest in the increased literary culture and general information of the students, and in their better prep-

Y. M. C. A. and Gymnasium Building.

aration for their forensic exercises. There is great lack of recent books in standard literature, history, science, biography. An urgent appeal is made to those who may be able to aid in supplying this lack. Recognition is due to those who have kindly contributed to the Library in the past year.

Among those to whom grateful acknowledgments are made are the Hon. H. R. Gibson, M.C., the United States Government, for many publications; Miss Amanda L. Andrews, Mrs. J. L. Godfrey, Mrs. Thaw and friends of the late Miss Linva A. Schenck, for a collection of books to her memory.

James R. Hills Library.

During the past nine years the students have enjoyed the privileges of the James R. Hills Memorial Loan Library. By a fund of six hundred dollars, generously contributed by Miss Sarah B. Hills, of New York, the College is enabled to rent the text-books used in the institution to those who cannot afford to buy them. The rate charged per term is one-fifth the wholesale price of each book. The income of rentals is devoted to supplying new books as they are needed. The usefulness of this library can hardly be overestimated.

John C. Branner Library.

A few years ago John C. Branner, Ph.D., then the State Geologist of Arkansas, gave another proof of his generosity and friendship to the College by establishing a Loan Library of the text-books used in the Natural Science Department. He contributed one hundred dollars for this purpose. The books in this library are under the same regulations as are those of the Hills Library.

The Misses Willard Library.

Through the generosity of the Misses Willard, of Auburn, N. Y., the text-book employed in the Bible classes is also provided for rent at a nominal charge.

Literary Societies.

The four Literary Societies connected with the institution are of the greatest benefit to those who faithfully avail themselves of the advantages they offer. The BAINONIAN, established in 1875, and the THETA EPSILON, established in 1894, are composed of young ladies; the ATHENIAN, established in 1868, and the ALPHA SIGMA, established in 1882, are composed of young men. These organizations have neatly furnished rooms —the BAINONIAN and the THETA EPSILON in the FAYERWEATHER ANNEX, the ATHENIAN and the ALPHA SIGMA in ANDERSON HALL—where they meet every Friday night to engage in debates and other literary exercises. All the societies give a public midwinter entertainment. During the past few years the ATHENIAN and the ALPHA SIGMA Societies have each sustained " Junior " Societies for the special benefit of the less

advanced students.   The ADELPHIC UNION LITERARY SOCIETY, which is
composed of the Societies already mentioned, gives an annual public entertainment during Commencement week.

Alumni Association.

This Association was formed in 1871, and holds its annual meeting
on Thursday of Commencement week.   The officers for the present year
are as follows : President, Rev. W. R. Dawson, '84 ; Vice-President,
Mrs. Emma E. Alexander, '75 ; Secretary, Prof. S. T. Wilson, '78·

Athletic Association.

This Association, organized to develop and systematize athletic sports
and gymnastic exercises, has had a prosperous year.   Manly men are
the leading spirits in the organization.   The officers are as follows :
President, Will T. Bartlett; Secretary, T. W. Belk ; Treasurer, Bert Ruble.

The foot-ball and base-ball teams have been equipped during the year
with new uniforms.   The new gymnasium, though only partially equipped,
has been of great service since it was opened to the students.   Field Day
was celebrated with enthusiasm on May 12.

Expenses.

The endowment enables the College to make its charges very moder-
ate.   Students rooming in the College buildings each pay for room rent
$3.00 per session, or $6.00 for the year.   The tuition bill is $6.00 per ses-
sion, or $12.00 for the year.   The heat bill in the halls is $3.00 per term.
The charge for electric lights is $1.00 for each term.   No other charges
except for music.   There are no incidental fees aside from a modest
laboratory fee.

No deduction will be made for absence at the beginning and the close
of the term.   College bills must be paid invariably in advance.   Until
this condition is complied with, no one can become a member of any of
the classes.   All students who room in Memorial Hall are required to
make a deposit of fifty cents with the Janitor.   This sum is a pledge that
the room taken will not be abused, and it will be returned to the student
at the end of the term if no damage has been done the room.

Washing, per term, will cost about $5.00 ; board in the Coöperative
Boarding Club costs per week about $1.25, while board in private
families, including furnished room, fuel, lights and washing, can be had
for from $2.00 to $3.00 per week.   The charge for instruction upon the
piano or organ, and for the use of the piano, is fixed at very reasonable
rates.   For the fall term, one lesson a week, $4.00 ; two lessons a week,
$8.00 ; for the second term, one lesson a week, $5.00 ; two lessons a
week, $10.00.   The Coöperative Boarding Club is spoken of below.

The rooms in Baldwin Hall are furnished with bedsteads, washstands
and tables.   The rooms in Memorial Hall are unfurnished.   Students
must supply their own bedding.

The entire expense for the students for board, tuition, room rent, fuel, light and washing, for the collegiate year, will be from $80.00 to $125.00.

This estimate is made on the supposition that two students occupy one room.

Students' Coöperative Boarding Club.

The Students' Coöperative Boarding Club, under the efficient charge of Mrs. A. A. Wilson, of the Mt. Nebo summer resort, has again been very successful in furnishing good board at a very low rate. The actual cost of the board is found at the end of each month, and the average price has been only $1.25 per week during the year. The students have shown their appreciation of the Club and more than one hundred and ninety have belonged to it. The young ladies have the privilege of doing a certain amount of work and receiving credit for it, thus materially reducing the cost of their board. It is doubtful whether any other College in the South can offer such good board at such low rates.

The Students' Fund.

Recognizing that one of the pressing needs of the College is scholarships, friends of the College continued the contributions which form what is called the Students' Fund. This money was placed at the disposal of the Faculty with the understanding that it should be used to help needy and deserving students, and those aided should work out the amount received upon the College grounds at the rate of seven and one-half cents per hour. Sixteen students during the year have earned money from this fund by doing faithful and conscientious work upon the *campus*. It is hoped that the friends of the College will become interested in this plan for aiding worthy students, and that the fund may be continued for the coming year.

The Carson Adams Fund.

This fund, amounting to about seven thousand dollars, was bequeathed to the College by the Rev. Carson W. Adams, D.D., of New York, who died October 12, 1887. "This fund is to be kept in perpetuity by the Trustees of said College, and to be called the CARSON ADAMS FUND. The income from it is to be expended in paying the tuition fees of indigent students, male or female." All applications for aid from this fund must be made in writing to the College authorities, and be accompanied by satisfactory proofs of character and of the needy circumstances of the applicants.

The George Henry Bradley Scholarship.

A scholarship of $1000, the income of which is to be used in aid of needy students, has been founded by Mrs. Jane Loomis Bradley, of Auburn, N. Y., to be called the "George Henry Bradley Scholarship," in memory of the only son of the donor and of the late Silas L. Bradley, President of the Bank of Auburn.

The Willard Scholarship.

The first of the twenty scholarships which the College is endeavoring to raise was a donation from the Misses Willard, of Auburn, N. Y., and the income has been employed most acceptably during the current year. This scholarship of $1000 serves to show once more the deep interest in Maryville College that is entertained by the generous donors. It is hoped that this may be followed by many such contributions in perpetual aid to worthy and needy students.

The Craighead Scholarship.

The income of a scholarship of $1500, given by the late Rev. James B. Craighead, D.D., is used in aid of young men studying for the ministry.

Prizes.

A gold medal has been offered by a friend to the student in the Freshman or Sophomore Classes in the Classical and Philosophical Courses, who shall have the highest average grade in the regular studies of the year. A gold medal has also been offered by Hon. Will A. McTeer to the student in the Preparatory Departments of the Classical and Philosophical Courses who shall have the highest average grade in the regular studies of his year. No student shall be eligible to compete twice for the same medal. These prizes will be conferred at the Commencement. The winners of the prizes last year were: College medal, William Houston Keeble; Preparatory medal, Dennis White Crawford.

The New Heating System.

A most complete and satisfactory system of heating and ventilating the College buildings has been installed at an expense of $10,000. All the rooms of Anderson Hall, Baldwin Hall, Memorial Hall and the Lamar Library are heated and ventilated by the "Fan" or Plenum System. A boiler-house has been built between Anderson and Memorial Halls, and in this house two sixty-horse-power boilers have been placed, together with a receiver and a pump for returning the condensed water to the boilers. Steam is carried in pipes placed under the ground to the basements of the different buildings, into batteries of radiators or coils of steam pipes placed closely together. Fresh air is driven over these coils of steam-heated pipes by means of a large fan operated by an engine, and the air thus heated is forced into galvanized iron pipes and distributed to the different rooms. Sufficient heated air is forced into every room to change the air in the room four times an hour, and ventilating ducts allow the vitiated air to escape. The action of this system does not depend upon atmospheric conditions, direction or force of the wind, and by forcing fresh, heated air under pressure to every room, uniform results are secured. This system of heating and ventilating not only diminishes the fire risk, but is conducive to health, especially to those who room in Memorial and Baldwin Halls.

Improvements.

Among the improvements recently made are a system of waterworks, by which pure water from a spring in the College grounds is carried throughout the different buildings; and the fitting up of a number of bathrooms in the two dormitories. Students do not have to carry water or fuel up flights of stairs.

Special Needs.

Some of the special needs of the College are the completion of the building for the use of the Y. M. C. A. and for a Gymnasium; equipments for the Department of Natural Sciences; scholarships to aid needy students, and books and endowment for the Lamar Memorial Library.

Bequests and Devises.

Since each State has special statutory regulations in regard to wills, it is most important that all testamentary papers be signed, witnessed and executed according to the laws of the State in which the testator resides. In all cases, however, the legal name of the corporation must be accurately given, as in the following form :

"I give and bequeath . . . . to the 'BOARD OF DIRECTORS OF MARYVILLE COLLEGE,' at Maryville, Tennessee, and to their successors and assigns forever, for the uses and purposes of said College, according to the provisions of its charter."

Synodical Examining Committee.

Revs. W. H. Lyle, D.D., John S. Eakin and John P. MacPhie compose the committee appointed by the Synod of Tennessee to attend the annual examinations of the College for the current year.

Terms and Vacations.

There are two terms in the Collegiate year, the first extending from the first of September to about the 23d of December, and the second from the first of January to the last Thursday of May.

Calendar for 1899=1900.

1899.
May   25, Commencement . . . . Thursday.
Sept. 5, Entrance Examinations. . . . . Tuesday.
Sept. 6, First Term begins. . . . . Wednesday.
Nov. 30, Thanksgiving . . . . Thursday.
Dec. 19, Examinations begin . . . . Tuesday.
Dec. 22, First Term closes. . . . . Friday.
1900.
Jan.   3, Second Term begins . . . . Wednesday.
Feb. 22, Washington's Birthday . . . . Thursday.
May   23, Examinations begin . . . . Wednesday.
May   27, Baccalaureate Sermon . . . . Sabbath.
May   27, Address before the Y. M. C. A. and Y. W. C. A Sabbath.
May   28, Address before the Adelphic Union. . . . . Monday.
May   29, Annual Exhibition of the Adelphic Union . . Tuesday.
May   29, Class Day Exercises. . . . . Tuesday.
May   30, Annual Meeting of the Directors, 9 A.M. . . . Wednesday.
May   30, The Senior Class Concert . . . . Wednesday.
May   31, Commencement . . . . Thursday.
May   31, Annual Meeting of the Alumni . . . . . . Thursday.
May   31, Social Reunion . . . . Thursday.

1899.   CALENDAR.   1900.

	S	M	T	W	T	F	S
SEPT.						1	2
	3	4	5	6	7	8	9
	10	11	12	13	14	15	16
	17	18	19	20	21	22	23
	24	25	26	27	28	29	30
OCT.	1	2	3	4	5	6	7
	8	9	10	11	12	13	14
	15	16	17	18	19	20	21
	22	23	24	25	26	27	28
	29	30	81				
NOV.				1	2	3	4
	5	6	7	8	9	10	11
	12	13	14	15	16	17	18
	19	20	21	22	23	24	25
	26	27	28	29	30		
DEC.						1	2
	3	4	5	6	7	8	9
	10	11	12	13	14	15	16
	17	18	19	20	21	22	23
	24	25	26	27	28	29	30
	31						

	S	M	T	W	T	F	S
JAN.		1	2	3	4	5	6
	7	8	9	10	11	12	13
	14	15	16	17	18	19	20
	21	22	23	24	25	26	27
	28	29	30	31			
FEB.					1	2	3
	4	5	6	7	8	9	
	11	12	13	14	15	16	
	18	19	20	21	22	23	24
	25	26	27	28			
MAR.					1	2	3
	4		6	7	8	9	10
	11		13	14	15	16	17
	18	5	20	21	22	23	24
	25	28	27	28	29	30	31
APRIL	1	2	3	4	5	6	7
	8	9	10	11	12	13	14
	15	16	17	18	19	20	21
	22	23	24	25	26	27	28
	29	30					
MAY			1	2	3	4	5
	6	7	8	9	10	11	12
	13	14	15	16	17	18	19
	20	21	22	23	24	25	26
	27	28	29	30	31		

CATALOGUE OF
MARYVILLE COLLEGE

....1899–1900....

CPSIA information can be obtained
at www.ICGtesting.com
Printed in the USA
BVHW091234261118
534010BV00012B/400/P

9 780656 786756